D1710406

FLAG DAY

HOLIDAY CELEBRATIONS

Jason Cooper

Rourke

Publishing LLC
Vero Beach, Florida 32964

www.rourkepublishing.com

PHOTO CREDITS: Cover, title page, p. 4, 10, 13 © Lynn M. Stone; p. 7 courtesy Betsy Ross House, Philadelphia; p. 8 courtesy of State Museum of Pennsylvania; p. 12, 14 © PhotoSpin; p. 17 © Harold Dobberpuhl; p. 18, 21 courtesy Library of Congress

Cover: *Children wave the American flag to celebrate Flag Day, June 14.*

Editor: Frank Sloan

Cover design by Nicola Stratford

Library of Congress Cataloging-in-Publication Data

Cooper, Jason, 1942-
  Flag Day / Jason Cooper.
      p. cm. — (Holiday celebrations)
Summary: An introduction to the history, purpose, and observance of Flag Day, when we honor our country's flag.
Includes bibliographical references and index.
  ISBN 1-58952-219-2 (hardcover)
  1. Flag Day—Juvenile literature. [1. Flag Day. 2. Holidays.] I.
Title. II. Holiday celebrations (Vero Beach, Fla.)
  JK1761 .C65 2002
  394.263--dc21   2002002388

Printed in the USA

TABLE OF CONTENTS

FLAG DAY

Flag Day honors the United States flag on June 14. America's first official flag was created by the **Continental Congress**. This took place in Philadelphia, Pennsylvania, on June 14, 1777.

Many people and businesses display American flags on Flag Day. Schools often have special events. On Flag Day people may discuss what the flag means and where it began. Some towns have parades or other **patriotic** events to celebrate Flag Day.

EARLY FLAGS

Today's 50-star flag looks different than the American flag of 1777 did. That flag was also red, white, and blue. But it had only 13 stars. **Congress** did not decide exactly how the stars on that flag should be arranged. Some flag makers put the stars in rows. Others put the stars in a half or full circle!

This is the Philadelphia home of Betsy Ross, who may have sewn the first official American flag.

THE STARS AND STRIPES

The U.S. flag is often called "Old Glory" or the "Stars and Stripes." The flag of 1777 had 13 stars and 13 stripes. Each star and stripe stood for one of the first 13 states.

The number of stripes on early flags, however, was not always the same. The famous flag that flew over Fort McHenry during the night of September 13-14, 1814, had 15 stripes! That flag, by the way, was the "Star Spangled Banner" that Francis Scott Key wrote about. His words became the National Anthem.

This painting shows Betsy Ross sewing an American flag in 1777.

ADDING STARS

In 1818 Congress decided that the flag would always have 13 stripes, one for each of the original states. Congress decided that each state would have a star. Stars have been added to the flag for each new state. The last stars were added in 1959 for Hawaii and Alaska.

A woman sews a modern American flag with 50 stars, one for each of the 50 states.

Flags decorate a bike at a Flag Day parade.

By waving American flags, schoolchildren celebrate Flag Day.

THE FLAG DAY FOUNDERS

The flag is a very important **symbol** to Americans. It stands for the ideals of the nation, such as **democracy** and **justice**. No one felt more strongly about this than Bernard J. Cigrand of Wisconsin. In 1877 Congress had asked that all public buildings fly the flag to honor the 100th birthday of the flag. But the idea of having a yearly Flag Day was the idea of Mr. Cigrand and a few other individuals.

The flag is a symbol of America's liberties, guaranteed by the U.S. Constitution.

We the People

MR. CIGRAND

Mr. Cigrand became a dentist and college dean. But in 1885 he was a 19-year-old schoolteacher. He taught in a country schoolhouse near Fredonia, Wisconsin.

The young teacher felt that the flag was important. It should be treated with the greatest respect. He began to make speeches and write articles about the flag. He continued to do so for the rest of his life.

The first celebration of Flag Day was in this country schoolhouse near Fredonia, Wisconsin.

EARLY FLAG DAYS

On June 14, 1885, Mr. Cigrand led his school in ceremonies to honor the flag's 108th birthday. The idea caught on.

In 1889 a kindergarten teacher, George Balch, held a Flag Day in his New York City school. On June 14, 1891, people at the Betsy Ross House in Philadelphia held a Flag Day celebration. Many people think Betsy Ross was the first person to sew an American flag.

Josephus Daniels speaks at a Flag Day rally in Washington, D.C., on June 14, 1914.

Other schools, towns, and organizations began to celebrate the flag on June 14. In 1893, Colonel J. Granville Leach suggested that Philadelphia make a great show of flags on June 14. He also suggested that June 14 be celebrated as Flag Day each year.

In 1949 President Harry S. Truman made Flag Day an official U.S. holiday.

A NATIONAL CELEBRATION

Flag Day exercises were held in Philadelphia's Independence Square on June 14, 1893. And in 1894 more than 300,000 schoolchildren in Chicago were part of Flag Day exercises.

After some 30 years of city and state Flag Days, in 1916 President Woodrow Wilson made Flag Day a national celebration. In 1949 President Harry Truman officially made June 14 Flag Day in the United States.

GLOSSARY

congress (CONG rus) — the body of elected senators and representatives who make laws for the U.S. Government in Washington, D.C.

Continental Congress (con tuh NEN tul CONG rus) — the lawmaking body of the 13 original colonies, from 1774 to 1789

democracy (dem OCK ruh see) — a government by the people and in which the majority rules

justice (JUSS tiss) — that which is fair, or just

patriotic (pay tree OT ick) — relating to the love of country

symbol (CIM bul) — an object, such as a flag, that stands for something, such as an idea or nation

INDEX

Further Reading

Ansary, Mir Tamim. *Flag Day*. Heinemann Library, 2001.

St. George, Judith. *Betsy Ross, Patriot of Philadelphia*. Henry Holt and
   Company, 1997

Websites To Visit

Flag Day Celebration at http:theholidayspot.com/flagday/history/celebration.htm

Flag History at http://www.geocities.com/Heartland/2328/flag.htm

http:www.flagday.org

About The Author

Jason Cooper has written several children's books about a variety of topics for Rourke
Publishing, including recent series *China Discovery* and *American Landmarks*. Cooper
travels widely to gather information for his books. Two of his favorite travel destinations
are Alaska and the Far East.